Research and Statistics in Social Sciences
Including Education

MCQ for Advanced Learners

S.K. Tyagi
Shanti Tejwani
Kaushalya Khatri

SHIPRA

(2014, First Published 2012)

Rs. 595

ISBN: 978-81-7541-652-9

2026 Impression, PoD

Research and Statistics in Social Sciences
MCQ for Advance Learners

Published by:
SHIPRA PUBLICATIONS
LG 18-19, Pankaj Central Market,
I.P. Ext., Patparganj, Delhi 110092, India
+91 11 47322068, 9650028065, 9810522367
info@shiprapublication.com
www.shiprapublication.com

Preface

The book contains two hundred Multiple Choice Questions followed with explanatory notes on various aspects of Research and Statistics in Social Science, particularly Education.

Admittedly, there are numerous standard text books on the subject, traditionally loaded with plenty of excercises towards the end of the chapters to test the learning of the readers. However, the conceptual understanding of the process of research, the repertory of skills a good researcher is supposed to have up his sleeves and the prudence to take appropriate decisions related to the conduct of research are not tested too frequently. Consequently, post graduate scholars intending to truly master the science and craft of social science research and those who wish to opt for M.Phil & Ph.D. research work with a view to eventually join the ranks of university/ college teachers by competing at national/state level eligibility test are left to grapple with their own meagre resources. The book seeks to extend a helping hand to such aspirants.

Furthermore, in pursuance to UGC's resolution of 2009, most of the Universities have already started making admissions to M.Phil/ Ph.D. course through an open entrance examination followed by successful completion of one semester of courseware in Research Methodology. The objectives of this designated course will need to be assessed and it is precisely for this purpose that the items of the book will come handy.

The content areas covered by the book are those which constitute major parts of the requirement of post graduate, M.Phil and Pre-Ph.D. courses in Social Sciences including Education. These include topics such as spelling out *Research Objectives, Formulation of Hypotheses, Research Designs, Nature of Data, Applicability of Parametric and Non-Parametric tests of Hypotheses, Interpretation of Results and the use of SPSS.*

Though utmost care has been taken in formulating the questions and proposing their solutions, it is probable that some errors might have inadvertently crept in. The authors shall be glad to promptly rectify such errors as are brought to their notice by the discerning readers.

Dr. S.K. Tyagi

Contents

MCQ

1. How many pair-wise comparisons are possible in case of six treatment groups?
   (a) 6
   (b) 3
   (c) 15
   (d) 30

2. Which of the following pairs is NOT appropriate?
   (a) Homogenous Population-Quota Sampling
   (b) Unknown Population-Cluster Sampling
   (c) Hidden Population-Snowball Sampling
   (d) Enumerable Population-Systematic Sampling

3. *Statement* I: The sum of adjusted means of different groups is equal to the sum of unadjusted means of the same groups.

   Statement II: The adjusted sum of square (total) is equal to the unadjusted sum of square (total).

   In the context of ANCOVA of equal sample size with one covariate the above two statements are respectively-
   (a) False, False
   (b) False, True
   (c) True, True
   (d) True, False

4. In a 3 × 2 × 4 Factorial Design ANOVA the number of interactional effects in all will be-
   (a) 24
   (b) 4
   (c) 6
   (d) 3

5. How many Sources of Variations will be there in a Three Way ANOVA?
   (a) 5
   (b) 6
   (c) 8
   (d) 7

6. A $2 \times 2 \times 2$ Factorial Design ANOVA is-
   (a) Two Way ANOVA
   (b) Three Way ANOVA
   (c) Eight Way ANOVA
   (d) Six Way ANOVA

7. Which one is the interpretation of significance of the main effect?
   (a) Whether taught by Lecture Method or by Film, Male students have significantly different achievement than Female students.
   (b) Male students taught by Lecture Method have significantly different achievement than Male students taught by Film.
   (c) Male students taught by Lecture Method have significantly different achievement than Female students taught by Lecture Method.
   (d) None of the above

8. Which of the following is an interpretation of the interactional effect between Gender and Method of Instruction?
   (a) Whether taught by Lecture Method or by Film, Male students have significantly different achievement than Female students.
   (b) Male students taught by Lecture Method have significantly different achievement than Male students taught by Film.
   (c) Male students taught by Lecture Method have significantly different achievement than Female students taught by Lecture Method.
   (d) None of the above

9. Which interpretation of the graph is NOT wrong?

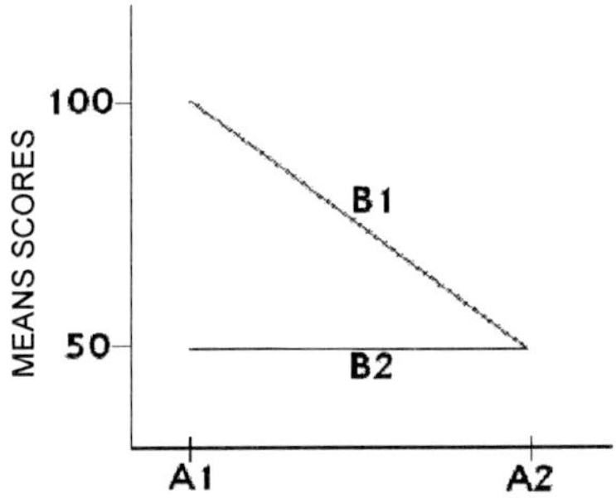

(a) A is significant but B and A × B are not significant.
(b) B is significant but A and A × B are not significant.
(c) A is not significant but B and A × B are significant.
(d) A, B and A × B all are significant.

10. Which of the graph is correct representation of situation where one of the main effect and interactional effect are significant?

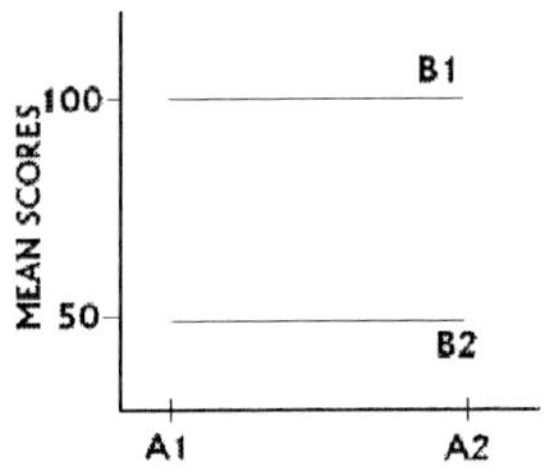

(a)

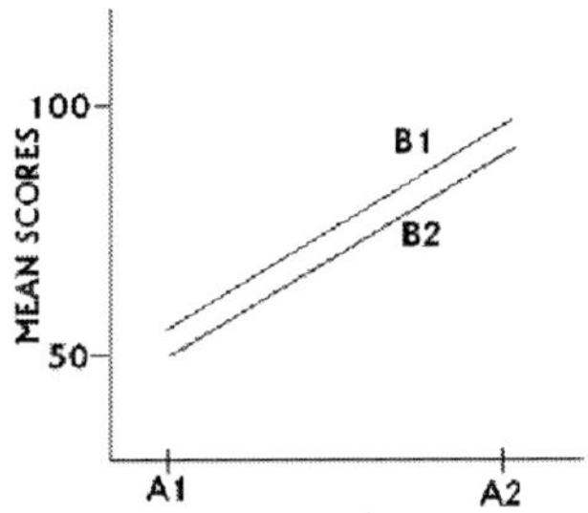

(b)

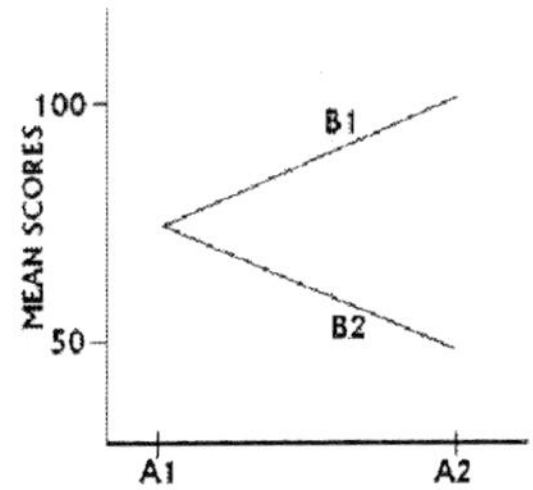

(c)

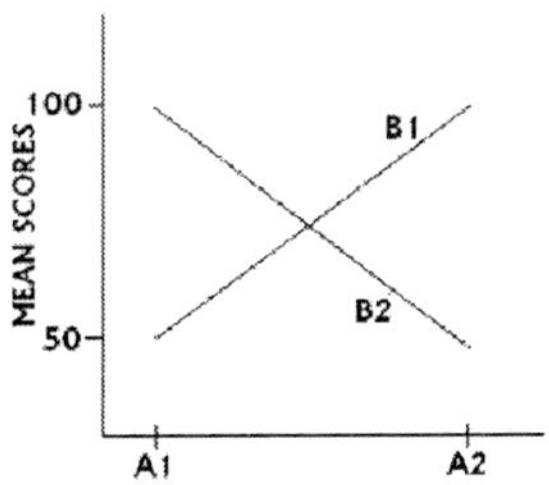

(d)

11. Pick up the correct one among the given statements.
    (a) In case of a non-significant F one or more t's can still be significant.
    (b) F cannot be significant without each t being significant.
    (c) F can be significant even if each t is not significant.
    (d) In case of a non-significant F, each t will also be non-significant.

12. Which one is the correct conclusion?
    (a) If H_0 is rejected at 0.01 level then it will also be rejected at 0.02 level of significance.
    (b) If H_0 is not rejected at 0.01 level then it will also not be rejected at 0.02 level of significance.
    (c) If H_0 is rejected at 0.02 level then it will also be rejected at 0.01 level of significance.
    (d) If H_0 is not rejected at 0.01 level then it will be rejected at 0.02 level of significance.

13. If probability of significance for a two-tailed test is 0.012 then H_0 will be-
    (a) Rejected at 0.05 level of significance
    (b) Not rejected at 0.05 level of significance
    (c) Rejected at 0.01 level of significance
    (d) Not Rejected at 0.02 level of significance

14. *Statement* I: Choosing higher level of significance increases the risk of committing β-error.

    Statement II: Probability of rejecting a false H_0 is more at a higher level of significance.
    (a) Statement I is true but Statement II is false.
    (b) Statement I is false but Statement II is true.
    (c) Both Statement I & II are true.
    (d) Both Statement I & II are false.

15. As compared to two-tailed test, a one-tailed test is more likely to-
    (a) Reject H_0 when it is true

(b) Not reject H_0 when it is true
(c) Not reject H_0 when it is false
(d) Reject H_0 when it is false

16. If probability (p) of significance for two-tailed test is 0.16, one tailed test will-
(a) Reject H_0 at 0.05 level of significance.
(b) Reject H_0 at 0.01 level of significance.
(c) Reject H_0 at 0.02 level of significance.
(d) Not reject H_0 at 0.01 level of significance.

17. At which level of significance a researcher is most likely to accept a false H_0?
(a) 0.01
(b) 0.001
(c) 0.02
(d) 0.05

18. Suppose four events A, B, C, and D are defined as follows-
(A) Rejecting a true H_0
(B) Rejecting a false H_0
(C) Not rejecting a true H_0
(D) Not rejecting a false H_0

If "p" denotes probability of event, then-
(a) p(A) + p(B)=1
(b) p(B) + p(D)=1
(c) p(C) + p(D)=1
(d) p(C) + p(B)=1

19. The shaded portion of the graph represents the probability of-

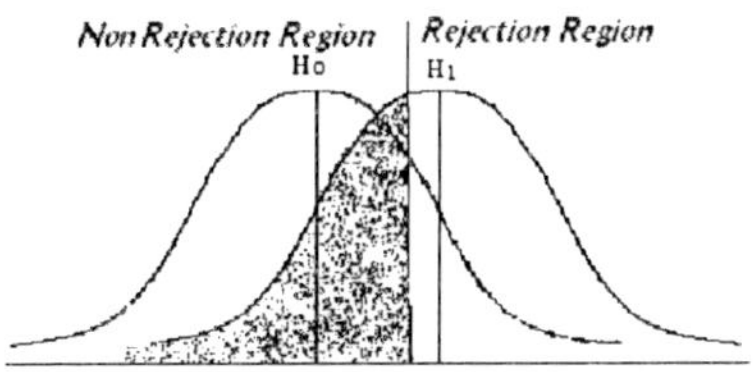

(a) Rejecting a true H_0
(b) Rejecting a false H_0
(c) Not rejecting a false H_0
(d) Not rejecting a true H_0

20. The shaded portion of the graph represents the probability of-

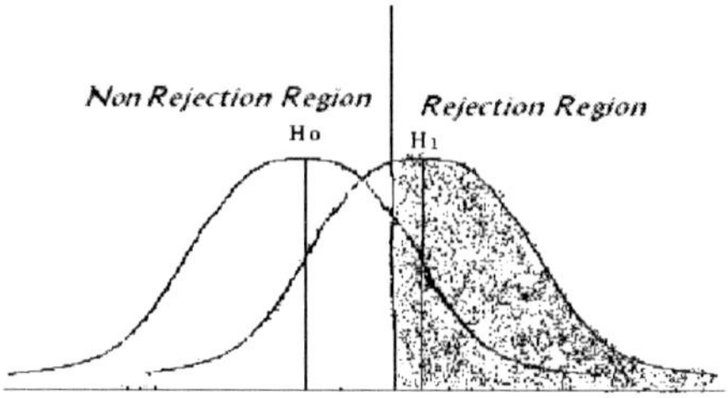

(a) Rejecting a true H_0
(b) Rejecting a false H_0
(c) Not rejecting a false H_0
(d) Not rejecting a true H_0

21. Separating H_1 and H_0 distribution apart will result in-
(a) Reducing both Type I and Type II errors.
(b) Increasing both Type I and Type II errors.
(c) Reducing Type I error but increasing Type II error.
(d) Increasing Type I error but reducing Type II error.

22. You want to compare mean scores of male and female adult population in respect of the following characteristics. Identify the characteristic for which t-test will not be justified.
(a) Income
(b) Intelligence
(c) Anxiety
(d) None of the above

23. Which of the following assumptions is NOT a must for the use of t-test?
(a) Randomization of sample
(b) Interval or Higher Scale data

(c) Normality of Distribution
(d) Equality of variances

24. Rejecting a H_0 at 0.02 level of significance means that-
(a) 98 per cent trials of the experiment will produce the same results.
(b) The deviation in results will be at the most 2 per cent.
(c) Individual differences will be within 2 per cent range.
(d) At the most 2 per cent trials, can give these results by chance only.

25. Which one is correct statement?
(a) Larger the sample size and larger the variability in scores, wider the confidence interval for population mean.
(b) Larger the sample size and larger the variability in scores, narrower the confidence interval for population mean.
(c) Larger the sample size and smaller the variability in scores, narrower the confidence interval for population means.
(d) Smaller the sample size and larger the variability in scores, narrower the confidence interval for population means.

26. Which pair of samples can be regarded as Correlated Samples?
(a) Pairs of Husband-Wife.
(b) Pairs of City-Village Dwellers.
(c) Pairs of Single Teacher-Multiple Teacher School.
(d) None of the above

27. The data related to which of the following variables do not permit use of One Way ANOVA?
(a) Educational Qualification
(b) Teaching Experience
(c) Attitude Towards Teaching
(d) Teacher Effectiveness

28. Identify the correct statement.
    (a) A two-tailed significance value of t is smaller than one-tailed significance value of t.
    (b) Two-tailed probability of significance is greater than one-tailed probability of significance.
    (c) For a balanced Two Way ANOVA
    $SS_{Total} \neq SS_A + SS_B + SS_{A \times B} + SS_{Error}$
    (d) Variances are homogenous if the ratio of greatest variance and the lowest variance is not significant.

29. Which one is correct formula for Sum of Square (SS)?
    (a) $\sum X^2$
    (b) $\frac{\Sigma X^2}{N}$
    (c) $\Sigma X^2 - \frac{\Sigma X^2}{N}$
    (d) $\Sigma X^2 - \frac{(\Sigma X)^2}{N}$

30. The value of F is-
    (a) Always positive
    (b) Always negative
    (c) Both positive and negative
    (d) None of the above

31. Which sample has variance different from the rest?
    (a) 5, 7, 6, 1, 2, 3, 4
    (b) 11, 41, 31, 71, 51, 21, 61
    (c) 61, 64, 67, 62, 63, 66, 65
    (d) – 7, – 2, – 5, – 6, – 4, – 3, – 1

32. Which one can be regarded as correlated sample?
    (a) Weights of teachers before and five years after marriage.
    (b) Income of farmers before independence and businessman after independence.
    (c) Interests of husbands and wives of Indore.
    (d) All the above

33. If two distributions are combined to make a pooled distribution then-
    (a) Pooled variance will be equal to individual variance.
    (b) Pooled variance will be equal to individual variance provided samples sizes are equal.
    (c) Pooled variances will be equal to individual variances provided group means are equal.
    (d) Pooled variances will be equal to individual variances provided both groups have equal sample size and equal means.

34. What can be concluded from the given graph?

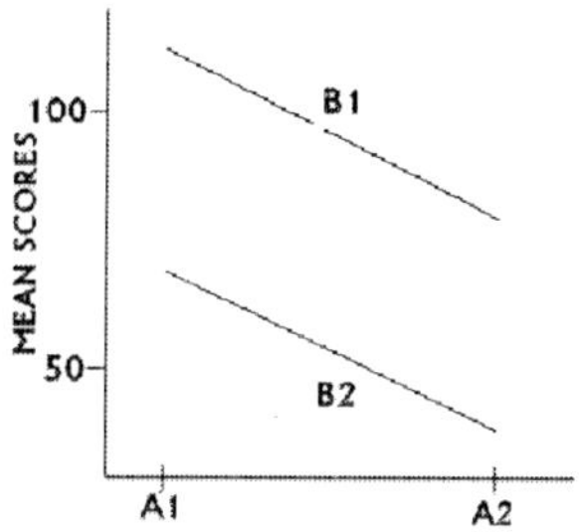

    (a) A and B are significant but A × B is not significant.
    (b) A is significant but B and A × B are not significant.
    (c) B is significant but A and A × B are not significant.
    (d) None of A, B, A × B significant.

35. Which statement is NOT correct for Two Way ANOVA of unequal cell size?
    (a) Weighted means instead of unweighted means are compared for testing significance of main effects.
    (b) $SS_{Total} \neq SS_A + SS_B + SS_{A \times B} + SS_{Error}$
    (c) $df_{Total} = df_A + df_B + df_{A \times B} + df_{Error}$
    (d) All the above

36. Which of the following will get a non-normal distribution?
    (a) Sports Talent among Sports person.
    (b) Stamina of Wrestlers.
    (c) Distance of a Shotput throw.
    (d) Daily Calorie Consumption of Cricketers.

37. In which situation will you reject H_o (two-tailed test) at 0.05 level of significance?
(a) $p = 0.10$
(b) $Z = -1.70$
(c) $p = 0.06$
(d) $p = 0.011$

38. Which expression is the correct one?
(a) $SS_{Subgroup} = SS_A + SS_B + SS_{A \times B}$
(b) $SS_{Within} = SS_{Subgroup} - (SS_A + SS_B)$
(c) $df_{A \times B} > df_A$ or (df_B)
(d) $SS_{A \times B} = SS_{Total} - SS_{Subgroup}$

39. SS_{Total} is usually equal to-
(a) $SS_{A \times B}$
(b) $SS_A + SS_B$
(c) $SS_A + SS_B + SS_{A \times B}$
(d) None of the above

40. For a 2 × 2 × 4 Factorial Design ANOVA of equal cell size of 5 subjects each, the df_{Error} will be-
(a) 16
(b) 64
(c) 80
(d) 65

41. Relationship between Item Response on an objective type test and total score on it, is studied through-
(a) r_{pbis}
(b) r_{bis}
(c) r_t
(d) ø

42. Relationship between an ordinal scale variable and an interval scale variable can be studied through-
(a) r_{bis}

(b) r_t
(c) ρ
(d) C

43. Association between Caste and Achievement levels can be studied through-
(a) r_t
(b) ø
(c) C
(d) ρ

44. Ø coefficient of correlation is most appropriate for which pair of the variables?
(a) Gender-Intelligence
(b) Gender-Item Response
(c) Gender-Educational Qualification
(d) Achievement level-Intelligence level

45. A 2 × 2 Table with underlying continuous variable will give-
(a) r_{pbis}
(b) r_t
(c) ø
(d) C

46. If one of the variables is on nominal scale while other is on ordinal scale, which correlation coefficient will be used?
(a) C
(b) Ø
(c) r_t
(d) ρ

47. If value of coefficient of correlation between the two variables is 0.9 then the commonness between them is-
(a) 90 per cent
(b) 10 per cent
(c) 81 per cent
(d) 91 per cent

48. Which assumption is most specific to Pearson correlation?
(a) Normality
(b) Homoscedasticity
(c) Randomness
(d) Linearity

49. Which value of correlation coefficient shows strongest relationship?
(a) –0.8
(b) +0.75
(c) –0.28
(d) 0.71

50. Which statement is wrong?
(a) $r_{XY} = r_{YX}$
(b) If $r_{XY}>0$ & $r_{YZ}<0$ then $r_{XZ}<0$
(c) If $r_{XY}=0$ & $r_{YZ}>0$ then $r_{XZ}>0$
(d) If $r_{XY}<0$ & $r_{YZ}<0$ then $r_{XZ}>0$

51. Which test CAN NOT do without the assumption of independence of samples?
(a) t-test
(b) F-test
(c) χ^2
(d) All the above

52. Which significant statistic can fall in either tail of the distribution?
(a) t
(b) F
(c) χ^2
(d) None of the above

53. Which table of frequency does not permit the use of χ^2?
(a)

	Yes	*No*
Male	10	12
Female	8	16

(b)

	Right	*Wrong*
#1	6	9
#2	5	11

(c)

	White	*Coloured*
Maruti	20	13
Indica	15	22

(d)

	Hit	*Missed*
Preferred Hand	8	21
Non-Preferred Hand	37	9

54. Which statement is NOT true for Yates' Correction?
(a) Yates Correction is used in case of any observed frequency being less than 5 but not less than 1
(b) Application of Yates Correction influences the computed value of χ^2
(c) Yates Correction is a must for a 2 × 2 table
(d) All the above

55. Chi-square test CAN NOT be used-
(a) For assessing the association between variables.
(b) To test the normality of a distribution.
(c) To test the observed percentage against a known percentage
(d) For studying independence of attributes.

56. Which among the following does not have a family of curves?
(a) t-distribution
(b) χ^2-distribution
(c) F-distribution
(d) Z-distribution

57. Choose the correct statement about χ^2 curves from those given below.
(a) Smaller the df, more the peak of curve moves to the right
(b) Larger the df, higher the peak of the curve
(c) Larger the df, farther the curve moves from normality
(d) Smaller the df, smaller the critical value of χ^2 to be significant at a particular level

58. $\chi^2 = 6$ was tested for significance and was found to be significant for some df at a particular level of significance. It means that $\chi^2 = 6$ will-
    (a) Be significant at a higher level of significance with same df
    (b) Not be significant at a lower level of significance with same df
    (c) Be significant at same level of significance with lesser df
    (d) Be significant at same level of significance with greater df

59. A calcutaled t-value when compared with table value with some df is found significant at 0.05 level of significance. It can-
    (a) Be significant at 0.05 level of significance even with quite smaller df
    (b) Not be significant at 0.10 level of significance with same df
    (c) Not be significant at 0.05 level with quite a greater df
    (d) None of the above

60. In a χ^2 test of independence A, B, C, D, E and F are cell frequencies as follows

A	B	C
D	E	F

The df for the contingency table is two as we are free to choose-
    (a) Any two of the six frequencies
    (b) The frequencies A & D
    (c) The frequencies C & F
    (d) The frequencies B & C

61. Which one is wrong option for question 60?
    (a) A & F
    (b) B & C
    (c) D & C
    (d) None of the above

62. Each of 100 subjects fall into any of the three categories: Disagree, Undecided and Agree. If the response is normally distributed, how many frequencies are expected in the category of Disagree?
    (a) 15
    (b) 20
    (c) 16
    (d) 25

63. Observed value of chi-square does not help in assessing-
    (a) Whether or not an observed distribution fits into a theoretical distribution
    (b) Where do differences lie in case of significance of the observed value
    (c) Whether or not given distribution deviates from normality
    (d) Whether or not every response category is equally likely

64. Which one is incorrect statement about critical value of chi-square?
    (a) $\chi^2_{0.05}(df = 30) < \chi^2_{0.05}(df = 10)$
    (b) $\chi^2_{0.05}(df = 10) < \chi^2_{0.01}(df = 10)$
    (c) $\chi^2_{0.05}(df = 15) < \chi^2_{0.02}(df = 15)$
    (d) $\chi^2_{0.10}(df = 15) > \chi^2_{0.10}(df = 10)$

65. Which one is a non-parametric test?
    (a) χ^2-test
    (b) t-test
    (c) Z-test
    (d) F-test

66. Which is the correct statement?
    (a) Parametric tests are not more powerful than their Non-parametric counterparts.
    (b) Observed frequencies in Chi-Square test do not add up to expected frequencies.
    (c) t-test is not a two-tailed test
    (d) Type I error and Type II error do not add up to one.

67. Which test requires the weakest assumptions?
    (a) Z-test
    (b) F-test
    (c) t-test
    (d) χ^2-test

68. Which is basically a test of goodness of fit?
    (a) F-test
    (b) χ^2-test
    (c) Correlated t-test
    (d) Z-test

69. Twelve male students of a sample agreed to a proposal while 8 showed their disagreement. Similarly, 28 females were in agreement and 52 in disagreement of the proposal. If the decision were independent of gender how many males are expected to agree on the proposal?
    (a) 8
    (b) 12
    (c) 20
    (d) 16

70. *Statement* I: χ^2 value is found to be significant. Standardised Residual for a particular cell is – 1.82; it means that there are significantly less observed values than the expected ones.

    Statement II: If χ^2 value is not significant then no cell will have significant Standardised Residual.
    (a) Statement I is false but Statement II is true.
    (b) Statement I is true but Statement II is false.
    (c) Both Statement I & II are false.
    (d) Both Statement I & II are true.

71. If observed & expected frequencies of any cell are 10 and 16 respectively then Standardised Residual is-
    (a) – 6
    (b) – 9
    (c) – 6/16
    (d) – 6/4

72. Which quantity is used in Residual analysis of Chi-Square?

(a) $\sqrt{f_o - f_e}$

(b) $\dfrac{(f_o - f_e)^2}{f_e}$

(c) $\dfrac{(f_o - f_e)^2}{\sqrt{f_e}}$

(d) $\dfrac{(f_o - f_e)}{\sqrt{f_e}}$

73. The quantity $(f_o - f_e)$ of a cell is called-

(a) Standardised Residual

(b) Residual

(c) Cell Contribution

(d) Cell Weight

74. Pick out the correct statement regarding Yates Correction?

(a) 0.5 is substracted from the residual before squaring it in case the residual is negative.

(b) 0.5 is added to the residual before squaring it in case the residual is negative.

(c) 0.5 is added to the residual before squaring it in case the residual is positive.

(d) None of the above

75. Students A & B are working on problems on χ^2. The value of χ^2 calculated by A (say c_A^2) was smaller than c_B^2. But c_A^2 was found to be significant, while c_B^2 was not significant. This could happen because-

(a) df with which A was working (df_A) was smaller than df_B

(b) The α-level with which B was working was lower than that of A.

(c) The N for the problem of student A was greater than for B.

(d) All the above

76. *Statement* I: Larger N means larger df for χ^2.

Statement II: Yates Correction need not be applied to case if $f_e > 5$.

(a) Both Statement I & II are false.
(b) Statement I is true but Statement II is false.
(c) Both Statement I & II are true.
(d) Statement I is false but Statement II is true.

77. Which symbol is a correct representation of Partial Correlation?

(a) $r_{1.23}$
(b) $r_{34.2}$
(c) $r_{23(1)}$
(d) $r_{1(23)}$

78. Which one represents Multiple Correlation?

(a) $R_{3(12)}$
(b) $R_{31.2}$
(c) $R_{3.12}$
(d) $R_{(31)2}$

79. Net correlation between two variables when the effect of third variable is partialled out ($r_{12.3}$) is-

(a) Greater than r_{12}
(b) Less than r_{12}
(c) Equal to r_{12}
(d) Either of the above

80. r_{12} will equal to $r_{12.3}$ when

(a) $r_{12} = 0$
(b) $r_{13} < 0$ and $r_{23} > 0$
(c) $r_{13} = 0$ and $r_{23} = 0$
(d) $r_{13} > 0$ but $r_{23} < 0$

81. Which formula for $r_{12.3}$ is correct?

(a) $\dfrac{r_{12} - r_{13}r_{23}}{\sqrt{1 - r_{12}^2}\sqrt{1 - r_{23}^2}}$

(b) $\dfrac{r_{12} - r_{13}r_{23}}{\sqrt{1 - r_{12}^2}\sqrt{1 - r_{13}^2}}$

(c) $\dfrac{r_{12} - r_{13}r_{23}}{\sqrt{1 - r_{13}}\sqrt{1 - r_{23}}}$

(d) $\dfrac{r_{12} - r_{13}r_{23}}{\sqrt{1 - r_{13}^2}\sqrt{1 - r_{23}^2}}$

82. The multiple correlation of a variable x with a combination of variables y & z is given by-

(a) $\sqrt{\left(1 - r_{xy}^2\right) + \left(1 - r_{xz}^2\right)}$

(b) $\sqrt{\left(1 - r_{xy}^2\right)\left(1 - r_{xz}^2\right)}$

(c) $\sqrt{1 - \left(1 - r_{xy}^2\right)\left(1 - r_{xz}^2\right)}$

(d) $\sqrt{1 - \left(1 - r_{xy}^2\right)\left(1 - r_{xz.y}^2\right)}$

83. Let 1 = Height, 2 = Weight, 3 = Intelligence. If r_{13} was found to be + 1 then what will be the value of $R_{1(32)}$?

(a) + 1
(b) 0
(c) Greater than 1
(d) Less than 1

84. Which expression(s) is/are NOT appropriate?

(a) $r_{12.3456}$
(b) $R_{1(234567)}$
(c) $R_{12(34)}$
(d) All the above

85. Which one is NOT the assumption of Partial Correlation?
   (a) Ordinal scale measurement
   (b) Homosedasticity
   (c) Continuity of variables
   (d) Normality of scores

86. If 1= Attitude towards Maths, 2 = Achievement in Maths and 3 = TV watching time then the value of $r_{12.3}$ will be –
   (a) Positive and less than r_{12}
   (b) Positive and greater than r_{12}
   (c) Positive but may be greater or less than r_{12}
   (d) Equal to r_{12}

87. Which test will be suitable for the situation having two Independent Variables with three levels of each and one Dependent Variable on which groups are to be compared?
   (a) Two Way ANOVA
   (b) Three Way ANOVA
   (c) Two Sample χ^2 test
   (d) None of the above

88. Which test is appropriate for analyzing the nominal scale data falling in the given categories below?

Before	*After*		
	Strongly Agree	*Agree*	*Undecided*
Strongly Agree			
Agree			
Undecided			

   (a) χ^2-test
   (b) McNemar test
   (c) Kendall's Coefficient of Concordance 'W'
   (d) None of the above

89. Median test is similar to which of the following tests?
   (a) Independent t-test
   (b) Correlated t-test
   (c) One Way ANCOVA
   (d) Two Way ANCOVA

90. The specific assumption of Factorial Design ANCOVA is-
    (a) Normality for Covariate
    (b) Homogeneity of Variance
    (c) Homogeneity of Regression Statistics
    (d) None of the above

91. Which test will be used to compare the Pre-and Post-tests ratings for five students given below?

Students	*Pre-test*	*Post-test*
A	1	3
B	2	3
C	2	5
D	5	4
E	4	6

    (a) Wilcoxon Matched Pairs Signed Ranks test
    (b) Correlated t-test
    (c) Sign test
    (d) None of the above

92. Which test is called for comparing the ranks of Male and Female students given below?
    Male: 1.5, 3, 8
    Female: 5, 4, 1.5, 7, 6
    (a) t-test
    (b) Wilcoxon Matched Pairs Signed Ranks test
    (c) Median test
    (d) None of the above

93. Non-Parametric alternative to One Way ANOVA is-
    (a) Friedman's Test
    (b) Kruskal Wallis Test
    (c) Repeated Measures ANOVA
    (d) Mann-Whitney U-Test

94. K-related samples with interval scale data will be treated with-
    (a) Friedman's Test
    (b) Single Factor ANOVA
    (c) Repeated Measures ANOVA
    (d) None of the above

95. Which coefficient of association will be used for the following data?

Ranks by Judges			
Objects	*X*	*Y*	*Z*
A	1	1	2
B	2	3	1
C	5	2	3
D	4	5	4
E	3	4	5

(a) Cramer's Coefficient
(b) Contingency Coefficient 'C'
(c) Spearman Coefficient 'ρ'
(d) Kendall's Coefficient of Concordance 'W'

96. The minimum requirement of Scale of data for Wilcoxon Matched Pairs Signed Ranks Test is:
(a) Ordinal Scale
(b) Interval Scale
(c) Ratio Scale
(d) Ordinal-Interval Scale

97. Which of the following is NOT true?
(a) Sign Test can also be used where McNemar's Test has been used.
(b) Sum of Squares for all effects may not equal to Total Sum of Square in Factorial Design ANOVA.
(c) Un-weighted Mean Analysis is used in the case of unequal sample size.
(d) None of the above.

Questions 98 to 106 contain one objective of research each. One of the four fragments of the objective has some technical error in it. Identify the erroneous fragment.

98. To compare(1)/the adjusted mean scores of frustration of(2)/undergraduate students of different residential backgrounds(3)/by considering sex as covariate.(4)
The erroneous fragment in the above research objective is:
(a) 1

(b) 2
(c) 3
(d) 4

99. To study (1)/the effect (2)/of Treatment, Gender and Medium of Instruction (3)/on the Achievement in Mathematics of Class IX students of Indore (4).
The fragment containing error is:
(a) 1
(b) 2
(c) 3
(d) 4

100. To compare (1)/the mean Pre-test and Post-test scores of (2)/Class XII students of Indore (3)/belonging to the Activity Method of Teaching English (4).
Which fragment has error in it?
(a) 1
(b) 2
(c) 3
(d) 4

101. To study (1)/the correlation between (2)/the Religious Affiliation of Civil Services Candidates and (3)/their aspired post (4).
Which fragment has error in it?
(a) 1
(b) 2
(c) 3
(d) 4

102. To study the effect of (1)/Treatment, Personality and their interaction (2)/on mean Verbal Flexibility scores of students of (3)/Senior Secondary Classes (4).
The erroneous fragment is:
(a) 1
(b) 2
(c) 3
(d) 4

103. To study the influence of (1)/Gender, Personality and their interaction(2)/on Exam Anxiety scores (3)/of Primary School Children (4).
Which fragment has error in it?
(a) 1
(b) 2
(c) 3
(d) 4

104. To study (1)/the effect of mean scores of (2)/Treatment, Gender and their interaction (3)/on Spatial Ability of Secondary students (4).
Which fragment is technically flawed?
(a) 1
(b) 2
(c) 3
(d) 4

105. To compare (1)/the mean Teacher Effectiveness scores (2)/of the three Teacher Training Module groups (3)/by taking Teaching Experience and Pre-Teacher Effectiveness as covariates (4).
The fragment containing technical error is:
(a) 1
(b) 2
(c) 3
(d) 4

106. To study the influence of (1)/Father occupation, Birth Order of the child and their interaction (2)/on Frustration (3)/by considering Intelligence scores as Covariate (4).
The erroneous fragment is:
(a) 1
(b) 2
(c) 3
(d) 4

107. Which of the following tests does not require the assumption of Independence of Observations?
(a) Sign Test

(b) t-test
(c) Kruskal-Wallis Test
(d) Mann Whitney U-Test

108. In One Way ANCOVA (N = 80) with four levels of Independent variable and two Covariates the degrees of freedom for main effect and the total will respectively be-
(a) 3 and 77
(b) 3 and 76
(c) 3 and 79
(d) 3 and 74

109. Cell means for a 2 × 2 ANOVA are given below:

	A_1	A_2
B_1	36	38
B_2	40	70

Which of the following is most likely to be true?
(a) Effect A is significant, effect B and effect A × B are not significant.
(b) Effect B is significant, effects A and A × B are not significant.
(c) Effects A and B are not significant, effect A × B is significant.
(d) All effects A, B and A × B are significant.

110. You are given two statements.

Statement I: In a Factorial Design ANCOVA cell means are not adjusted for the covariate.

Statement II: A variable to be considered as covariate must be measured on at least Interval Scale.

Choose the correct alternative from below:
(a) Both statements I and II are false.
(b) Both statements I and II are true.
(c) Statement II is false but not statement I.
(d) Statement I is false but not statement II.

111. Which of the following research objectives is most appropriate?
  (a) To compare Pre-test and Post-test scores of Achievement of Boys and Girls of class VII.
  (b) To compare mean scores of Achievement in Pre-test and Post-test of Boys and Girls of Class VII.
  (c) To study the effect of Treatment, Gender and their interaction on Achievement of Class VII students.
  (d) To compare mean scores of Achievement of Class VII of (a) Boys and Girls (b) Pre-test and Post-test separately.

112. *Statement* I: A non-directional hypothesis is called null hypothesis.

  Statement II: Estimated Marginal Means (Adjusted Means) are not used in ANOVA in the absence of covariate.

  Choose the correct alternative from below:
  (a) Both statements I and II are false.
  (b) Both statements I and II are true.
  (c) Statement II is false but not statement I.
  (d) Statement I is false but not statement II.

113. "There is no significant association between Caste of the B. Ed. students and their Grades in Course 503."
  Which of the following will be used to analyse the data related to the hypothesis given above?
  (a) Chi-Square
  (b) Contingency Coefficient
  (c) Kendall's Coefficient
  (d) Phi-Coefficient

114. Ordinal Scale data with two factors will be treated with-
  (a) Friedman Two Way ANOVA by Ranks
  (b) Mann Whitney U-Test
  (c) Wilcoxon Matched Pairs Signed Ranks Test
  (d) None of the above

115. Interval Scale data related to four levels of an Independent variable alongwith two Covariates will be analysed with the help of –
   (a) 4 × 2 Factorial Design ANOVA
   (b) Two Way ANCOVA
   (c) One Way ANCOVA
   (d) None of the above

116. Frequency data cast in 3 × 4 Contingency table is amenable to treatment by-
   (a) Two Way ANOVA by Ranks
   (b) K-sample Chi-Square Test
   (c) Two Sample Chi-Square Test
   (d) Cochran Q-Test

117. Ranking data about ten subjects from three judges can be analysed by using-
   (a) Kendall's Coefficient
   (b) Contingency Coefficient
   (c) Chi-Square Test
   (d) Friedman's Test

118. Repeated Measures in dichotomies from a sample can be treated with-
   (a) Cochran Q Test
   (b) Friedman's Test
   (c) Chi-Square Test
   (d) McNemar's Test of Significance of Change

119. "To compare mean Pre-Test and Post-test scores of Originality, Flexibility and Elaboration separately of B. Ed. students"
   Which of the test will be used to analyse the data related to the above objective?
   (a) One Way ANCOVA
   (b) Repeated Measure ANOVA
   (c) Paired Sample t-test
   (d) Wilcoxon Signed Ranks Test

120. Which test will be appropriate to analyse the data related to the following research objective?
"To study the effect of Treatment, Gender, Caste and their interactions on Attitude towards Mathematics of Class XII students"
(a) Two Way ANOVA
(b) Three Way ANOVA
(c) Three Way ANCOVA
(d) Two Way ANCOVA

121. Which hypothesis is the most appropriate for two samples Chi-Square Test?
(a) There are equal chances of rural and urban students making right or wrong response.
(b) There is no significant difference in Rural and Urban, Right and Wrong Responses.
(c) The Right and Wrong Responses of Rural and Urban students do not differ significantly.
(d) Residential Background of students is not significantly associated with their Responses.

122. Yates' Correction for Continuity is NOT applied when-
(a) No $f_e < 5$ and df = 1
(b) All $f_e > 5$ for a 2 × 2 Contingency Table
(c) df > 1 and No $f_e < 5$
(d) df = 1 or some $f_e < 5$

123. Which combination gives a situation that does NOT require an application of Yates' Correction for Continuity?

A_1-All	B_1-$f_e<5$	C_1-and	D_1-df=1
A_2- Some	B_2-$f_e>5$	C_2-or	D_2-df>1

(a) $A_1B_2C_1D_1$
(b) $A_1B_2C_1D_2$
(c) $A_2B_1C_2D_1$
(d) $A_2B_2C_2D_2$

124. Which Sum of Squre (SS) does not use Haromonic Mean of sample sizes in case of counter-balanced design?
   (a) $SS_{\text{Interaction}}$
   (b) $SS_{\text{Main Effects}}$
   (c) SS_{Within}
   (d) SS_{Subgroup}

125. Sample Sizes for each cell in 2 × 2 Factorial Design ANOVA are given below-
   $nA_1B_1 = 10$
   $nA_1B_2 = 5$
   $nA_2B_1 = 8$
   $nA_2B_2 = 20$

   What is the Harmonic Mean of the four sample sizes approximately?
   (a) 8.4
   (b) 10.8
   (c) 9.8
   (d) 7.4

126. In A × B × C Factorial Design ANOVA with three levels of A, two levels of B and four levels of C, the degree of freedom for the interaction A × B is-
   (a) 6
   (b) 4
   (c) 2
   (d) 3

127. Degrees of Freedom for an Independent t-test can be fractional in the case of –
   (a) Equal N, unequal variances
   (b) Equal N, equal variances
   (c) Unequal N, unequal variances
   (d) Unequal N, equal variances

128. The data in terms of Ranks of a group of students in two school subjects can be treated with-
    (a) Rank Difference Correlation
    (b) Matched Pairs Signed Ranks Test by Wilcoxon
    (c) Sign Test
    (d) McNemar's Test of Change

129. The Interval Scale data related to Single Group Pre-Test-Post-Test Design can be analysed using-
    (a) t-test
    (b) Paired Sample t-test
    (c) One Way ANCOVA
    (d) Sign Test

130. Which test is suitable for treating the interval scale data of Experimental Group Control Group Pre-Test Post-Test Design?
    (a) Two Way ANOVA
    (b) Paired Sample t-test
    (c) Two Way ANCOVA
    (d) One Way ANCOVA

131. The interval scale data of Parallel groups Post-Test only Design is amenable to –
    (a) Paired Samples t-test
    (b) One Way ANOVA
    (c) Independent Samples t-test
    (d) None of the above

132. The dichotomous data from Single Group Pre-Test-Post-Test Design can be analysed with-
    (a) Correlated t-test
    (b) McNemar Test of Change
    (c) Wilcoxon's Signed Ranks Test
    (d) None of the above

133. The Scale data of an experiment with Time Series Design can be analysed with-
    (a) Trend Analysis

(b) Friedman Analysis
(c) One Way ANOVA
(d) One Way ANCOVA

134. The data arising out of Soloman Four Group Design is amenable to treatement by-
(a) Factorial Design ANOVA
(b) One Way ANCOVA
(c) One Way ANOVA
(d) Factorial Design ANCOVA

135. A test of differences among groups for Scale data obtained from single sample with three replicates is-
(a) Correlated t-test
(b) A series of correlated t-test
(c) One Way ANCOVA
(d) Repeated Measure ANOVA

136. If p denotes significance value for a mean difference, which of the following statements is incorrect in the context of various Post-hoc Tests?
(a) $p_{Bonferroni} > p_{LSD}$
(b) $p_{Scheffe} < p_{Bonferroni}$
(c) $p_{Duncan} > p_{LSD}$
(d) $p_{Duncan} < p_{Scheffe}$

137. If α-level for one comparison is 0.05 what is the value of α for family of three comparisons?
(a) $1 - (0.05)^3$
(b) $1 - (1 - 0.05)^{1/3}$
(c) $1 - (1 - 0.05)^3$
(d) $[1 - (1 - 0.05)]^{1/3}$

138. A researcher compares mean differences among five groups. The significance of one of such difference is found to be 0.006. After controlling for α-inflation, this difference is-
(a) significant at 0.01 level of significance
(b) Significant at 0.006 level of significance

(c) Significant at 0.05 level of significance
(d) Not significant at 0.05 level of significance

139. In a family of eight comparisons if α level is set at 0.01 level of significance then α correction for Family Wise Error will be-
(a) (0.01)/28
(b) 0.01 × 28
(c) 0.01 × 8
(d) 0.01 × 16

140. Bonferroni test is applied for pairwise comparisons among family of 6 groups means. One of the mean difference yields a significance value of 0.72. The uncorrected p-value of significance for this difference will be-
(a) 0.072
(b) 0.12
(c) 0.432
(d) 0.012

141. Which of the following statement is false?
(a) $Z = \pm 1.96$ means two-tailed significance probability, $p<0.05$
(b) Two-tailed significance probability $p=0.001$ means the value$|Z|>2.58$
(c) $|Z|>1.65$ means two-tailed significance probability $p<0.05$
(d) All the above

142. *Statement* I: Type I error means rejecting a null hypothesis

Statement II: Type II error means failure to reject a null hypothesis
(a) Both statements I and II are false.
(b) Both statements I and II are true.
(c) Statement II is false but not statement I.
(d) Statement I is false but not statement II.

143. If the table gives the probability of one-tailed significance of the statistics as 0.09 then the formulated null hypothesis should-
(a) Be rejected at 0.05 level of significance
(b) Be rejected at 0.01 level of significance
(c) Not be rejected at 0.05 level of significance
(d) Be rejected at 0.09 level of significance

144. Z-value for some statistics was found to be 2.38, the correct decision is
(a) Not to reject null hypothesis at 0.05 level of significance
(b) Not to reject null hypothesis at 0.01 level of significance
(c) To reject null hypothesis at 0.01 level of significance
(d) To reject null hypothesis at 0.05 level of significance

145. If t-value for a difference between means was found to be more than the table value of t for 0.01 level of significance (with appropriate df) then the difference is interpreted to be-
(a) Significant at both 0.05 level and 0.01 level of significance
(b) Significant at 0.05 level but not significant at 0.01 level
(c) Significant at 0.01 level but not at 0.05 level
(d) Significant at 0.01 level of significance

146. The term "Adjusted Standardised Residual" is related to –
(a) Correlated t-test
(b) ANCOVA
(c) Factorial ANOVA
(d) Chi-Square Test

147. *Statement* I: Mann Whitney U-Test can be applied to Ordinal Scale data.

Statement II: Wilcoxon Matched Pairs Signed Ranks Test can not be applied to Ordinal Scale data.
(a) Both statements I and II are false.
(b) Both statements I and II are true.
(c) Statement II is false but not statement I.
(d) Statement I is false but not statement II.

148. t-test is related to ANOVA in exactly the same way as Residual Analysis is related to-
    (a) Chi-Square
    (b) Factor Analysis
    (c) Paired Samples t-test
    (d) ANCOVA

149. ANOVA is related to t-test in exactly the same way as Kruskal-Wallis Test is related to-
    (a) Friedman's Test
    (b) McNemar's Test
    (c) Mann Whitney U Test
    (d) Wilcoxon's Signed Ranks Test

150. Identify the pair different from the rest.
    (a) Wilcoxon Matched Pairs Signed Ranks Test and Correlated t-test
    (b) Repeated Measure ANOVA and Friedman Two Way ANOVA by Ranks
    (c) One Way ANOVA and Kruskal Wallis Test
    (d) Two Sample Chi-Square Test and McNemars Test of Significance of Change

151. Which of the following test is odd one out?
    (a) Sign Test
    (b) McNemar's Test
    (c) Chi-Square Test
    (d) Wilcoxon Matched Pairs Signed Ranks Test

152. Which one of the following test is different from the lot?
    (a) Kolgomorov Test
    (b) Chi-Square Test of Goodness of Fit
    (c) Shapiro-Wilk Test
    (d) Levene's Test

153. "Girl students of Class IX have significantly higher mean scores of Science Achievement than Boy students" is an example of a-
    (a) Positive Hypothesis

(b) Directional Hypothesis
(c) Both (a) and (b)
(d) None of the above

154. "Rural Graduate students are not as Anxiety ridden as their urban counterparts" is an example of-
(a) Positive Hypothesis
(b) Negative Hypothesis
(c) Directional Hypothesis
(d) Null Hypothesis

155. Parametric technique to analyse the data for between group effects obtained from K-related samples is-
(a) Repeated Measure ANOVA
(b) K-Way ANCOVA
(c) Trend Analysis
(d) Repeated Measure ANCOVA

156. Parametric technique to analyse the data for within group effects obtained from K-related samples is-
(a) Repeated Measure ANOVA
(b) K-Way ANCOVA
(c) Trend Analysis
(d) Repeated Measure ANCOVA

157. Which of the following statements is NOT incorrect?
(a) A non-directional hypothesis is null hypothesis.
(b) A null hypothesis is a statistical hypothesis.
(c) A statistical hypothesis is a declarative hypothesis.
(d) All the above

158. In the context of research report, what does 'Notes' mean?
(a) An explanatory reference
(b) An expository text
(c) A referred source used in the text
(d) Related literature used in the text

159. *Statement* I: There is significant difference between Intelligence and Creativity.

Statement II: Null hypothesis is a hypothesis of no difference between two variables
(a) Both statement I and II are correct.
(b) Statement II is incorrect but statement I is correct.
(c) Statement II is correct but statement I is incorrect.
(d) Statement II is incorrect and statement I is also incorrect.

160. "To study the relationship between Intelligence and Adjustment of Senior Secondary students"
The variable 'Intelligence' in the above objective is-
(a) Independent variable
(b) Dependent variable
(c) Covariate
(d) None of the above

161. A researcher conducts an experiment on Achievement of students. He takes two groups, one of which is given reinforcement while learning but the other is not. Pick up the most appropriate hypothesis to be tested under the given circumstances.
(a) There is no significant relationship between reinforcement and Achievement
(b) Reinforcement and Achievement have zero correlation
(c) Whether Reinforcement is given or not, the Achievement of both groups is same
(d) All the above

162. Null hypothesis is a statement of-
(a) No difference between two groups
(b) No relationship between two variables
(c) No difference between two variables
(d) No relationship between two groups

163. Which statement is most appropriate description of an Independent variable?
(a) It is controlled by the researcher.
(b) It is not related to other variables.
(c) It does not help anyone in research.
(d) It works independently in research.

164. A Covariate-
   (a) Affects the Independent variable of a research study.
   (b) Affects the Dependent variable of a research study.
   (c) Mixes with other variables and develops relationship with them.
   (d) Associates with obstructions in research.

165. Which type of research is likely to have the following research objective?
   "To study the influence of Gender, SES and their interaction on the Exam Anxiety of tenth graders"
   (a) Casual-Comparative research
   (b) Experimental research
   (c) Developmental research
   (d) Correlational research

166. "To compare the mean scores of Hindi of Fifth graders belonging to various groups on the basis of Duration of Examination"
   Which type of research is likely to have the above research objective?
   (a) Casual-Comparative research
   (b) Experimental research
   (c) Developmental research
   (d) Correlational research

167. "To compare mean scores of Creativity of Rural, Urban And Semi-urban students of Indore"
   Which type of research is likely to have above research objective?
   (a) Casual-Comparative research
   (b) Experimental research
   (c) Developmental research
   (d) Correlational research

168. "To compare mean scores of Reading Comprehension before and after introduction of Optical Devices of students belonging to Central Vision Loss and Peripheral Vision Loss separately"

Which kind of research is likely to have the above research hypothesis?
(a) Casual-Comparative research
(b) Experimental research
(c) Developmental research
(d) Correlational research

169. Which research design will be used to test the hypothesis related to the research objective of Q. No. 168?
(a) Pre-test-post-test design
(b) Parallel group design
(c) Parallel group pre-test-post-test design
(d) Pre-test-post-test Single Group Design

170. Which research design underlies the McNemar's Test of Significance of Change?
(a) 2 × 2 Factorial Design
(b) 2 × 2 Contingent frequency design
(c) Single group tested twice
(d) Two groups tested twice

171. For a given level of significance the two-tailed rejection region is as follows-

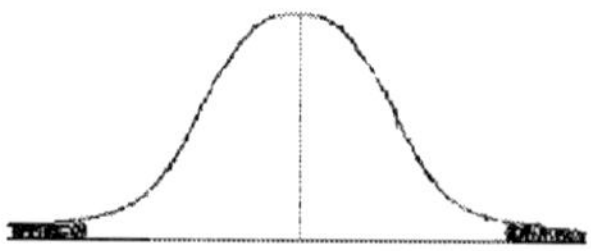

Which will be corresponding one tailed rejection region?

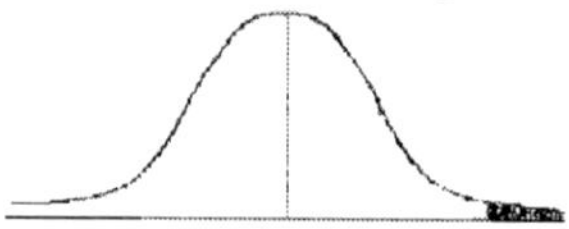

(a)

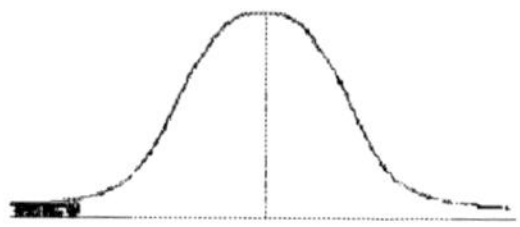

(b)

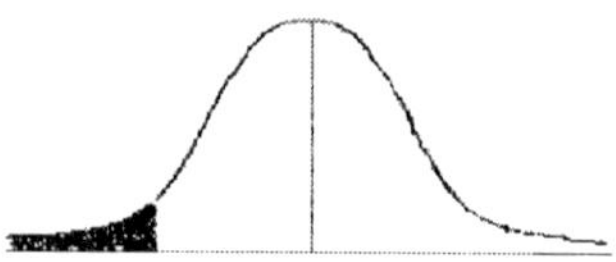

(c)

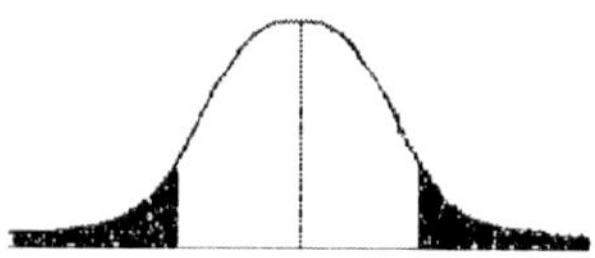

(d)

172. Which of the following tests takes into consideration the individual differences within groups?
    (a) Both F and t-tests
    (b) Only F-test
    (c) Only t-test
    (d) Neither F nor t-test

173. "There is no significant difference between Intelligence and Creativity." What is appropriate about this statement?
    (a) It is a null hypothesis because it declares no difference.
    (b) It is a null hypothesis because it declares no difference between two variables.
    (c) It is a not a null hypothesis because it declares difference between two variables.
    (d) It is a not a null hypothesis because it is not declaration of relation between two variables.

174. Which is the true statement about Independent Variable from the following statements?
    (a) It is out of control.
    (b) It does not affect anyone.
    (c) It is not affected by anyone.
    (d) Independence of any variable is a relative.

175. Which is the true statement about Covariate?
    (a) It has good relation with others.
    (b) It works in cooperative way.
    (c) It affects dependent variable.
    (d) It affects Independent Variable.

176. Pick up the true statement about Criterion Variable.
    (a) It is a kind of Dependent Variable.
    (b) It has high value.
    (c) Not giving proper attention on it results in punishment.
    (d) It has its own criteria.

177. Out of the following statements which statement is NOT true?
   (a) Independent Variable is of special and of its own type of variable.
   (b) Independent Variable are measured on at least Interval Scale.
   (c) Intervening variable are out of control.
   (d) All the above.

178. "There is a significant relationship between Intelligence and Creativity." Based on the above hypothesis which statement is true?
   (a) It is a null hypothesis in which Intelligence is an independent variable.
   (b) It is not a null hypothesis but Intelligence is an Independent variable.
   (c) It is a null hypothesis in which Creativity is a dependent variable.
   (d) It is not a null hypothesis and Creativity is also not a dependent variable.

179. "There is a significant effect of Reinforcement Design on Performance."
   The above hypothesis is a-
   (a) Directional Null Hypothesis.
   (b) Non-Directional Null Hypothesis.
   (c) Directional Alternative Hypothesis.
   (d) Non-Directional Alternative Hypothesis.

180. Which variables are related to changes in dependent variable?
   (a) Independent Variable, Covariate and Intervening Variables.
   (b) Independent and Intervening Variables.
   (c) Independent and Concurrent Variables.
   (d) Independent Variable.

181. Which Variable can be controlled after Experiment?
   (a) Concurrent Variable.
   (b) Concomitant Variable.

(c) Dependent Variable.
(d) Criterion Variable.

182. "There is no significant correlation between Intelligence and Creativity." In the above statement-
(a) Intelligence is an Independent Variable but Creativity is Dependent Variable.
(b) Intelligence is Dependent Variable but Creativity is an Independent Variable.
(c) Both Intelligence and Creativity are Independent Variables.
(d) Neither Intelligence nor Creativity is an Independent Variable.

183. Only Nominal Scale measure is used for this variable.
(a) Covariate
(b) Criterion Variable
(c) Independent Variable
(d) Intervening Variable

184. The External Validity of an experiment is threatened by which kind of variable?
(a) Criterion Variable
(b) Covariate
(c) Intervening Variable
(d) Independent Variable

185. The Regression Coefficients of Y on X and the Regression Coefficient of X on Y-
(a) Are equal and have same signs.
(b) Are equal and have opposite signs.
(c) Need not be equal but shall have same signs.
(d) Need not be equal but shall have opposite signs.

186. If b denotes the Regression Coefficient of Y on X and b' denotes the Regression Coefficient of X on Y, then the relationship between the two Coefficients is given by-
(a) $b + b' = r^2$
(b) $b/b' = r^2$
(c) $(bb')^2 = r^2$
(d) $bb' = r^2$

187. The Regression Coefficient of Y on X-
   (a) Can not be zero.
   (b) Can not be negative.
   (c) Can not be greater then one in absolute terms.
   (d) None of the above

188. If $\tilde{Y}$ and $\overline{Y}$ denote the Predicted and Mean value of Y respectively, which of the following expresses Residual Sum of Square?
   (a) $\Sigma(Y-\overline{Y})^2$
   (b) $\Sigma(\tilde{Y}-Y)^2$
   (c) $\Sigma(\tilde{Y}-\overline{Y})^2$
   (d) None of the above

189. Identify the term denoting Regression Sum of Square?
   (a) $\Sigma(\tilde{Y}-Y)^2$
   (b) $\Sigma(Y-\overline{Y})^2$
   (c) $\Sigma(\tilde{Y}-\overline{Y})^2$
   (d) None of the above

190. *Statement* I: If Regression Equation of Y on X is Y = –1.5 + 0.5X, then Regression Equation of X on Y will be X = 2Y + 3

   Statement II: If Regression Equation of X on Y is X = Y, then Regression Equation of Y on X will be Y = X
   Which of the following options is correct?
   (a) Both the statements I and II are true.
   (b) Statement I is true but statement II is false.
   (c) Both the statement I and II are false.
   (d) Statement I is false but statement II is true.

Q. 191 – 196:

Scatter plot of five ordered pairs (X_i, Y_i) shown by the symbol * is given below. Answer Question based on it.

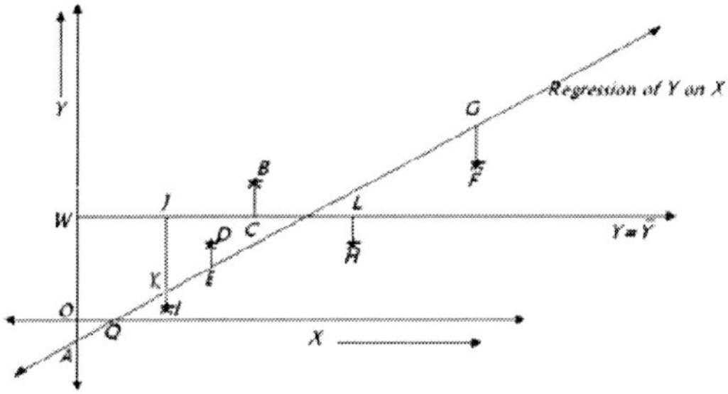

191. Which of the following shows neither Predicted value of Y nor Actual value of Y?
   (a) A
   (b) C
   (c) H
   (d) G

192. Which of the following does NOT show the Predicted value of Y?
   (a) Q
   (b) A
   (c) I
   (d) G

193. Which of the following distances is not relevant to the Residual Sum of Square?
   (a) HL
   (b) IK
   (c) DE
   (d) GF

194. Which of the following distances is relevant to the Residual Sum of Square?
   (a) KJ
   (b) IJ
   (c) DE
   (d) BC

195. Which of the following is the constant term of the Regression Equation of Y on X?
   (a) OQ

(b) AW
(c) OW
(d) OA

196. If Y = a + bX be the Regression Equation (shown in figure) of Y on X, then which of the following is true?
(a) a is negative, while b is positive.
(b) a is negative and b, too, is negative.
(c) a is positive while b is negative.
(d) a is positive and so is b.

197. Identify the incorrect statement in the context of Simple Linear Regression.
(a) All Predicted values lie on Regression Line.
(b) All Actual values lie on Regression Line provided Regression Coefficient is unity.
(c) The constant term of the Regression Equation does not depend upon the Regression Coefficient.
(d) Smaller the Residual Sum of Square, greater the chances of significance of Regression effect.

198. In case the Regression Line coincides with the line $Y = \bar{Y}$, which of the following will not be true?
(a) $SS_{Residual} = 0$
(b) r = 0
(c) xy = 0
(d) $SS_{Regression} = 0$

199. *Statement* I : If N is given and $t_{calculated} < t_{tabulated}$ (one-tailed), then H_o will be rejected in favour of the Directional Hypothesis.

Statement II : The constant term being zero, the Predicted value of Y at X will be zero.
The above statements in that order are respectively-
(a) True, True
(b) True, False
(c) False, True
(d) False, False

200. The mean score of the Dependent variable for a group will be adjusted upwards if the mean score of the covariate for the same group is-
    (a) Smaller than the total mean of the covariate and the correlation coefficient is negative.
    (b) Smaller than the total mean of the covariate while the correlation coefficient is positive.
    (c) Greater than the total mean of the covariate and the correlation coefficient is positive.
    (d) None of the above.

ANSWERS KEY

Q.	Ans.	Q.	Ans.	Q.	Ans.
1.	(c)	33.	(d)	65.	(a)
2.	(b)	34.	(a)	66.	(d)
3.	(d)	35.	(a)	67.	(d)
4.	(b)	36.	(c)	68.	(b)
5.	(c)	37.	(d)	69.	(a)
6.	(b)	38.	(a)	70.	(c)
7.	(a)	39.	(d)	71.	(d)
8.	(d)	40.	(b)	72.	(d)
9.	(d)	41.	(b)	73.	(b)
10.	(c)	42.	(c)	74.	(d)
11.	(a)	43.	(c)	75.	(a)
12.	(a)	44.	(b)	76.	(a)
13.	(a)	45.	(b)	77.	(b)
14.	(a)	46.	(a)	78.	(a)
15.	(d)	47.	(c)	79.	(d)
16.	(d)	48.	(d)	80.	(c)
17.	(b)	49.	(a)	81.	(d)
18.	(b)	50.	(c)	82.	(d)
19.	(c)	51.	(c)	83.	(a)
20.	(b)	52.	(a)	84.	(c)
21.	(a)	53.	(d)	85.	(a)
22.	(a)	54.	(a)	86.	(b)
23.	(d)	55.	(a)	87.	(a)
24.	(d)	56.	(d)	88.	(d)
25.	(c)	57.	(d)	89.	(a)
26.	(a)	58.	(c)	90.	(c)
27.	(a)	59.	(d)	91.	(c)
28.	(d)	60.	(d)	92.	(c)
29.	(d)	61.	(d)	93.	(b)
30.	(a)	62.	(c)	94.	(c)
31.	(b)	63.	(b)	95.	(d)
32.	(a)	64.	(a)	96.	(d)

Q.	Ans.
97.	(d)
98.	(d)
99.	(c)
100.	(b)
101.	(b)
102.	(c)
103.	(c)
104.	(b)
105.	(b)
106.	(d)
107.	(a)
108.	(a)
109.	(d)
110.	(b)
111.	(c)
112.	(a)
113.	(b)
114.	(d)
115.	(c)
116.	(c)
117.	(a)
118.	(a)
119.	(c)
120.	(b)
121.	(d)
122.	(c)
123.	(b)
124.	(c)
125.	(a)
126.	(c)
127.	(c)
128.	(a)
129.	(b)
130.	(d)
131.	(c)

Q.	Ans.
132.	(b)
133.	(a)
134.	(d)
135.	(d)
136.	(d)
137.	(c)
138.	(d)
139.	(a)
140.	(b)
141.	(c)
142.	(a)
143.	(c)
144.	(d)
145.	(d)
146.	(d)
147.	(b)
148.	(a)
149.	(c)
150.	(d)
151.	(c)
152.	(d)
153.	(b)
154.	(c)
155.	(a)
156.	(c)
157.	(c)
158.	(a)
159.	(d)
160.	(d)
161.	(c)
162.	(a)
163.	(a)
164.	(b)
165.	(a)
166.	(b)

Q.	Ans.
167.	(a)
168.	(b)
169.	(d)
170.	(c)
171.	(c)
172.	(a)
173.	(c)
174.	(d)
175.	(c)
176.	(a)
177.	(d)
178.	(d)
179.	(d)
180.	(a)
181.	(b)
182.	(d)
183.	(c)
184.	(b)
185.	(c)
186.	(d)
187.	(d)
188.	(b)
189.	(c)
190.	(b)
191.	(b)
192.	(c)
193.	(a)
194.	(c)
195.	(d)
196.	(a)
197.	(c)
198.	(a)
199.	(d)
200.	(b)

EXPLANATORY NOTES

1. (c) Suppose six treatment groups are 1, 2, 3, 4, 5, 6. There will be 15 pairwise comparisons as follows –

Pairs (1,2), (1,3), (1,4), (1,5) & (1,6)	= 5
Pairs (2,3), (2,4), (2,5) & (2,6)	= 4
Pairs (3,4), (3,5) & (3,6)	= 3
Pairs (4,5) & (5,6)	= 2
Pairs (5,6)	= 1
Total	= 15

2. (b) Since cluster sampling is random sampling among clusters.

3. (d) Statement I is true as if one group mean is adjusted upward, the other (s) are adjusted downward to that extent only. Adjustments are made to SS_{total} also, so statement II is false.

4. (b) There will be four interactional effects, namely AxB, AxC, BxC and AxBxC.

5. C) As there will be 3 main effects, 4 interactional effects and one within group effect.

6. (b) There are three factors with two levels of each, so it will be three way ANOVA.

7. (a) Since it talks about one gender being better in achievement than the other irrespective of method of teaching.

8. (d) Since each of the other alternatives is about main effects. (Gender in (a), Method of Instruction for males in (b), and Lecture method for Genders in (c))

9. (d) Due to inordinately high mean score for A_1B_1 from A_1B_2, A_2B_2 & A_2B_1 respectively, all the effects namely A, B and AxB are significant.

10. Let us examine each option:
    (a) B_1 means are higher for both levels of A_1 & A_2 as compared to B_2 means. So B effect is significant. Also interaction is absent.
    (b) A_2 means for both levels of B_1 & B_2 are higher as compared to A_1 means. So, A effect is significant. No interaction effect is seen as graph consists of parallel lines.
    (c) A effect is significant as well as AxB is significant.
    (d) None of A or B is significant, although AxB is significant.
    Hence answer is (c).

11. (a) This can happen due to increase in α-error while testing multiple hypotheses. This is why conducting a number of t-tests without performing F-test is inadvisable.

12. (a) As α is a lower level than α if H_0 happens to be rejected at 0.01 level, it must also be rejected at 0.02 level.

13. Since probability of significance $p = 0.012$ is not less than 0.01, H_0 cannot be rejected at $\alpha = 0.01$ level, Also $p=0.012 <.05$, hence H_0 deserves rejection at 0.05 level. So answer is (a).

14. Choosing higher level of significance (α) decreases α-error but at the same time increases risk of β error. Hence, statement I is correct. Probability of rejecting a false hypothesis is power of the test which is $(1-\beta)$. As β-error is more at higher level of significance, probability of rejecting a false H_0 are less. So, statement II is false. Accordingly, answer is (a).

15. In one tailed test, a smaller value of statistic is required to reject a hypothesis. So, one tailed tests are more powerful than two tailed tests. Hence, they are more likely to reject H_0 when it is false.
    Answer thus is (d).

16. (d) Since p=0.16 for a two tailed test, so for one tailed test p=0.08. Hence, the test will not reject H_0 at 0.01 level of significance. ($p>\alpha$).

17. (b) Since higher the α-level, higher the β-error, α=0.001 is most likely to accept the H_0 when it is false.

18. (b) As you either reject or not reject a false hypotheses, p(B) + p (D)=1.

19. The shaded portion is a part of H_1 curve (i.e. H_0 is false) and a non rejection region. Thus it represents "Not rejecting a false H_0".
Accordingly, answer is (c).

20. (b) "Rejecting a false H_0". As again the shaded part is of H_1 curve but this time it is in rejection region. It is also called power of the test.

21. (a) If H_1 and H_0 are separated from each other, the portion of H_0 to the right of rejection line (α-error) as well as the portion of H_1 curve to the left of rejection line (β-error) will get shrunk. Hence, both errors will be reduced.

22. (a) Income. Mean scores of income cannot be compared as income is not normally distributed among adult population.

23. (d) The assumptions equality of variance is not a must for t-test. The formula for t in such situation is as follows.

$$t = \frac{D}{Sp\sqrt{\frac{1}{N_1}+\frac{1}{N_2}}}$$

$$Sp = \sqrt{\frac{(N_2 - 1)s_1^2 + (N_2 - 1)s_2^2}{(N_1 - 1) + (N_2 - 1)}}$$

where s_1^2, s_2^2 are two sample variances

D = Difference between two sample means of size N_1 and N_2.

24. (d) α-level represents the probability of chance occurrence. α=0.02 in percentage is 2 per cent.

25. As the Confidence interval is M ± t σ_M, its width depends on σ_M. Since $\sigma_M = \frac{\sigma}{\sqrt{N-1}}$, smaller σ, larger N will produce narrower margin.
So answer is (c).

26. (a) Since the selection of husband in one selects the wife in another.

27. (a) Because Educational Qualification will yield nominal scale data, unsuitable for ANOVA.

28. (d) Since every other statement is wrong.

29. (d) Sum of Square (SS) is Σx^2 i.e. Sum of squares of deviation from mean. Further, as $\Sigma x^2 = \sum X^2 - \frac{(\Sigma X)^2}{N}$, the answer is (d).

30. (a) The value of F ratio is always positive as it is ratio of two positive quantities i.e. Sum of Squares

$$F = \frac{SS\ Between\ groups}{SS\ within\ groups}$$

31. Note that variance is independent of order. Also adding/Substracting a constant does not change variance but multiplication of each score by a constant affects variance. Each (c) score is 60 more than (a) score. Also each (a) score is 8 more than (d) score. Thus (a), (b) and (d) distributions have identical variance. (b) scores are obtained from (a) scores by first multiplying with 10 and adding 1, so the variance gets different. Hence answer is (b).

32. (a) As the scores refer to same subjects measured at two points of time.

33. (d) Between group variance is zero because of equality of means and also the sample sizes are equal. So pooled variance will be average of individual variances.

34. (a) B_1&B_2 lines are parallel indicating no significant interaction between A&B. Further, the two lines are separated from each other as well as slant, indicating significance of both A and B effects.

35. (a) Weighted means i.e. means based on all observations are not used in Factorial Design ANOVA of unequal cell size. Instead unweighted means i.e. means of cell means are compared.

36. (c) The distribution will be positively skewed. Most of the scores will be situated towards the left.

37. (d) Since only p=0.011<.05, the other given p-values are greater than 0.05, also Z= – 1.7 falls short of – 1.96, hence not significant.

38. (a) All other expressions are incorrect as:
   (i) $SS_{Subgroup}$-$(SS_A + SS_B) = SS_{AxB}$, so (b) is false.
   (ii) $df_A + df_B = df_{AxB}$
   in case $df_A = 1$, $df_B = 1$
   $df_{AxB} = 1$] So (c) is false
   (iii) $SS_{total} - SS_{Subgroup} = SS_{within}$, so (d) is false

39. (d) None of the above. As usually

$$SS_{total} = SS_A + SS_B + SS_{AxB} + SS_{within}$$

40. b) This is Three Way ANOVA with N=(2 × 2 × 4) × 5 =80 subjects

$$\begin{aligned} df_{error} &= df_{total} - (df_A + df_B + df_C + df_{AxB} + df_{BxC} + \\ &\quad df_{CxA} + df_{AxBxC}) \\ &= 79 - (1 + 1 + 3 + 1 + 3 + 3 + 3) \\ &= 79 - 15 = 64 \end{aligned}$$

$$\begin{aligned} \text{Note-}df_A &= 1,\ df_B = 1, \&\ df_C = 3 \\ df_{AxB} &= 1 \times 1 = 1 \\ df_{BxC} &= 1 \times 3 = 3 \\ df_{CxA} &= 3 \times 1 = 3 \\ \&\ df_{AxBxC} &= 3 \end{aligned}$$

41. (b) Since the vaiable "response to an item" is dichotomized and total score is an interval scale variable, r_{bis} is the appropriate.

42. (c) As interval scale variable can be reduced to ordinal scale variable and the coefficient of correlation for two ordinal scale variables is spearman rho (ρ).

43. (c) As both caste and Achievement levels are nominal scale variables with more than two categories, contingency coefficient (c) will be most appropriate.

44. (b) Because ϕ coefficient is applicable when both variables are genuine dichotomies, which Gender & Item Response are.

45. (b) r_t is the right choice because both the variables have been dichotomized.

46. (a) As the ordinal scale variable can always be reduced to a nominal scale variable.

47. (c) The commonness of variance shared between two variables is given by $r^2 = (.9)^2 = 0.81$ or 81 per cent.

48. (d) Pearson's coefficient is about relationship between two variables and the term specifically related with this is 'linearity'.
    So, answer is (d).

49. (a) As strength of relationship is given by quantity and the sign tells about the type, (a) is the answer.

50. (c) Let us see all options:
   (a) is true as r is reflexive
   (b) is also true as X and Y vary in the same direction but Y&Z vary in the opposite direction. So, X & Z will vary in the opposite directions.
   (d) if X increases, Y decreases and decreasing Y means increasing Z. So increase in X is associated with increase in Z. Thus $r_{xz} < 0$. So (d) is true
   (c) False, as X & Z will not vary together in any direction.

51. (c) As t & F tests have their correlated versions whereas the Chi square test requires independent samples.

52. (a) Since t distribution has two tails. Also, F and Chi square have no negative values, thus possess tails in positive side only (right hand).

53. (d) Since all other samples arc independent samples but in (d) preferred & non-preferred hands are of the same subject i.e each subject takes chance first by one hand, then the other. Thus the two observations are not independent of each other and hence chi square is precluded.

54. (a) Yates correction is applied when fe < 5 and no fe < 1.

55. (a) Chi square test is a test of hypothesis, not a measure of association like contingency coefficient.

56. (d) Z-distribution is unique, without a family. All others have different shaped curves for relevant degrees of freedoms.

57. (d) Note that the critical values in any column of chi square table increases as we go down. That is, larger values are required to be significant with increasing df. The other three statements are obviously false once one looks at a chi square family of curves.

58. (c) for the same reasons as given in the previous question.

59. Note that

    (i) In t-table if we go down in any column (i.e. increase N) The critical values of t gets smaller, and

    (ii) Values of t given in the table increase as we go from left to right (i.e increase the level of significance)

    Now (a), (b) & (c) are all false in the light of the above.

    Answer, accordingly, is (d).

60. (d) Choosing frequencies A & D is wrong option. As (A + D) is given, you need to choose either A or D, not both. So (b) is false. For same reasons (c) is false. Since (b) & (c) are false (a) is false. The correct option is (d), because as B & C are chosen A is determined. D, E & F are, too, determined.

61. (d) None of the above is wrong as:

A determines D, F determines C, A & C determine B, B determines E. Similar for options (b) & (c).

62. (c) The category 'Disagree' will consist of the area below M-1σ. Since between M and M-1σ there are 34.13 per cent cases in a normal distribution, the area falling under 'Disagree' will be 15.87 per cent i.e 16 per cent. Thus the frequencies will be 16.

63. (b) In case chi-square value is significant it tells that there are differences between observed and expected frequencies overall. The exact locations of the significant differences are identified by examining Standardised Residuals.

64. (a) Critical value of $\chi^2_{0.05}$ df (30) will be greater than $\chi^2_{0.05}$ df (10) because with increased df greater values of chi square are required to be significant. The other (b) and (c) are true as with a given df, lower the significance level, lower the critical value. Also, (d) is true.

65. (a) Chi-square test is non-parametric as it uses nominal scale data and fewer assumptions are required.

66. (d) Type II error and Type I error do not add upto 1. Other statements are true.

67. (d) Being a non-parametric test it requires minimal assumptions.

68. (b) A goodness of fit test tells us how close one distribution is to the another. Chi square is one such statistical test.

69. The problem can be worked out in the following manner. The observed frequencies are:

	Agree	*Disagree*	*Total*
Male	12	8	20
Female	28	52	80
Total	40	60	100

If decision were independent of Gender, the expected frequencies for the cell, "Male Agree" will be:

$$fe = \frac{Product\ of\ Margianl\ Sums}{Total\ Frequency}$$

$$= \frac{20X40}{100} = 80$$

So, the answer is (a)

70. (c) Let us examine each statement & see how?

I: Standardised residual is $\frac{fo - fe}{\sqrt{fe}}$ and is interpreted like a Z-value. Since its value for a cell falls short of 1.96, it cannot be therefore concluded that there are significantly less observed frequencies than the expected ones. Therefore statement I is false.

II: If Chi square value is not significant, some of the cells may give significant standardised residuals. This is similar to situation having a non-significant F-value alongwith some of the significant t-values due to α-inflation. So statement II is also false.

So the key is (c) i.e. False, False.

71. (d) Since Standardised Residual =(fo-fe)/ $\sqrt{fe}$

$$\frac{10-16}{\sqrt{16}} = \frac{-6}{4}$$

72. (d) Residual Analysis use the expression (fo-fe)/ $\sqrt{fe}$

73. (b) (fo-fe) is called Residual

74. (d) In case of Yates correction $(fo\text{-}fe)^2$ is replaced by $(|fo\text{-}fe| - 0.5)^2$ in the formula for chi-square, where (fo-fe) is the residual. In the light of this, none of (a), (b) or (c) is correct. So, answer is (d).

75. (a) Since a smaller value of chi square is needed to be significant for a smaller df. Thus statement (a) is true.

76. (a) Larger N need not give larger χ^2. Also, Yates correction is applied in case fe<5 in not more than 20 per cent of the cells and not less than one in any cell.

77. (b) Partial correlation is correlation between two variables keeping another variable (s) constant. So the correct symbol is $r_{34.2}$. The variable after dot represents the one which has been partialled out.

78. (a) Multiple correlation is correlation between one variable and a combination of two or more variables. Hence correct representation given option is $R_{3(12)}$. The variables within brackets means they have been taken in combination.

79. (d) The net correlation between two variables, say 1 and 2 when the effect of third variable, say 3 is partialled out depends on r_{12}, r_{23} and r_{13}. The quantity $r_{12.3}$ may be less than greater or equal to r_{12}.

80. (c)

$$Since\ r_{123} = \frac{r_{12} - r_{13}\, r_{23}}{\sqrt{1 - r_{13}^2}\,\sqrt{1 - r_{23}^2}}$$

$r_{12.3}=r_{12}$, in case $r_{23}=0$ and $r_{13}=0$. Hence the answer is (c).

81. (d) The correct formula is given in the preceding explanation.

82. (d) is the correct formula.

83. (a) As $R_{1(32)} = \sqrt{1 - \left(1 - r_{13}^2\right)\left(1 - r_{12.3}^2\right)}$

If $r_{13} = 1$

$$R_{1(32)} = \sqrt{1 - 0} = 1$$

84. (c) Since (a) represents partial correlation between variables 1 & 2 by partialling out effects of variable 3,4,5 &6. Also (b) indicates multiple correlation between variable 1 and a combination of 2,3,4,5,6&7 Expression (c) is in appropriate.

85. (a) Partial correlation requires at least interval scale measures.

86. (b) Since $r_{12.3} = \frac{r_{12} - r_{13}r_{23}}{\sqrt{1 - r_{13}^2}\,\sqrt{1 - r_{23}^2}}$

Also, r_{12} is positive and also r_{13} is negative (intelligent ones spend less hours in study as compared to less intelligent). Hence $r_{12.3}$ will be positive and greater than r_{12}.

87. (a) Two way ANOVA, since there are two independent variables and one dependent variable. Dependent variable has to be on at least interval scale.

88. (d) Since the design is before-after, observations are not independent as required by chi square, thus precluding (a). Also, McNemar test is applicable when there are dichotomies, which is not the case here. Kendal's coefficient

of concordance needs ordinal scale data for computing coefficient of concordance. That leaves (d) as the answer to the problem.

89. (a) Because median test requires data from two independent groups.

90. (c) Interaction graph of covariate for different levels of each factor should be parallel.

91. (c) Wilcoxon matched pairs signed ranks test cannot be applied as it requires known differences between pre and post test measures. Correlated t-test too requires interval scale data with moderate sample size, both lacking in the given example.
As sign test just requires direction of change from pre to post test, the answer is (c)

92. (c) Correlated t-test cannot be applied on ranking data, so (b) is not the answer. Although, Wilcoxon's matched pairs signed ranks test is about two paired samples but it requires interval scale data. Sign test can tell whether posttest ratings are improvement on pretest ratings, so (c) is the answer.

93. (b) Non parametric test related to be K-independent samples is Kruskal Wallis Test.

94. (c) Repeated Measure ANOVA is the answer. Friedman's test is for ordinal scale data while single factor ANOVA is for interval data from k independent samples.

95. (d) Cramers Coefficient as well as Contingency Coefficient require independent observations. Spearman's ρ is for data from two related samples. K-related samples case is dealt with Kendals Coefficient 'W'.

96. (d) Ordinal-interval scale, as differences between scores must be ranked.

97. (d) As all the statements (a), (b) &(c) are true, none is false,

so answer is (d).

98. (d) Sex is a nominal scale variable and hence cannot serve as covariate.

99. (c) Fragment (3) must contain the term 'and their interactions'.

100. (b) The name of dependent variable does not occur in fragment (2).

101. (b) Both variables being measured on nominal scale, instead of the term correlation, association must be used.

102. (c) The fragment (3) should be 'on Verbal Flexibility of Students'. The word 'mean' and 'scores' are redundant.

103. (c) 'On Exam Anxiety' is the correct expression.

104. (b) It should be 'The effect of' rather than 'the effect of mean scores of'.

105. (b) The word 'adjusted mean' should replace mean in fragment (2)

106. (d) 'Scores' should not occur in fragment (4)

107. (a) As sign test deals with related samples.

108. (a) Since df for main effect is 4 – 1=3. Total df will be (N – 1)-No. of covariates i.e. (80 – 1) – 2 = 77.

109. (d) There will be significant difference in A_1 and A_2 means averaged over B_1 and B_2. Similarly, there will be significant difference between B_1 and B_2 means. Also, due to inordinately high A_2 B_2 mean (70), There will be significant interaction between A & B.

110. (b) Note that Factorial Design ANCOVA tests the difference

between adjusted means for main effects only. Hence I is true, so is II.

111. (c) Option (a) is inappropriate as it does not mention the word 'mean'. Also option (b) would have been correct if 'boys and girls' were omitted, (d) Would be correct if post test scores of boys and girls were compared by taking pre test as covariate. Hence (c) is the answer.

112. (a) Non-directional hypothesis need not be null hypothesis as there can be a non-directional alternative hypothesis. Also, in unbalanced ANOVA (unequal sample size) unweighted means are used which are also termed as Estimated marginal means.

113. (b) Chi-square is not a measure of association but a test of hypothesis. Kendals Coefficient requires ordinal scale data whereas phi coefficient needs data in dichotomies. Contingency coefficient can be computed for nominal scale data.

114. (d) There is no test given in the list capable of doing the task.

115. (c) As there is just one factor with covariates.

116. (c) Because there are just two samples/variables with three and four levels each.

117. (a) Kendalls coefficient is precisely used in such situations.

118. (a) Data in Dichotomies for repeated measures is analysed with Cochran Q test.

119. (c) We need to apply three paired samples t-tests each for Originality, Flexibility and Elaboration respectively.

120. (b) It is Three Way ANOVA as there are three main effects and no covariate.

121. (d) Since all others are inappropriate.

122. (c) If all cells have expected frequency greater than five and there are more than two cells we need not apply Yates correction.

123. (b) For the reasons listed above.

124. (c) SS_{Within} is calculated using actual means as in counter-balanced design, SS_{Total} is not sum of all effects of the model.

125. (a) The Harmonic mean of 10, 5, 8, 20 is the reciprocal of means of their reciprocals i.e.

$$\frac{4}{\frac{1}{10}+\frac{1}{5}+\frac{1}{8}+\frac{1}{20}} = \frac{4}{\frac{8+16+10+4}{80}} = \frac{4}{\frac{28}{20}} = 8.4$$

126. (c) Since $df_{AxB} = df_A \text{ x } df_B$

$$= (3-1) \times (2-1)$$
$$= 2$$

127. (c) Adjustments in df are made for interpreting significance of t when variance and means are unequal.

128. (a) As Wilcoxon test requires scores not ranks, other tests listed are also not suitable for given data.

129. (b) One Way ANCOVA is used in pre-test post-test design when there are atleast two groups. Hence paired sample t-test meant for two related samples, is the answer.

130. (d) Because Two Way ANOVA requires two factors and independent observations. Paired sample t-test is for replicated measures related to single sample or matched pairs. Two Way ANCOVA is not called for because of relatedness & single factor.

131. (c) Since there are two independent groups and one criterion variable.

132. (b) McNemar's test is employed for dichotomous data from two related samples.

133. (a) Trend analysis is the appropriate statistical technique for analysing changes in criterion variable over different points of time.

134. (d) Soloman four group design is pre-test-post-test experimental treatment design to which three more groups are added: one without treatment, second without pre-test and the third without of pre-test and treatment. Its data analysis is complex and involves a number of techniques.

135. (d) In case of Interval scale data with more than two replicates, the test used is Repeated Measure ANOVA.

136. (d) $\mathbf{p}_{\text{Scheffe}} > \mathbf{p}_{\text{Duncan}}$ as Scheffe test is most conservative i.e. least powerful.

137. (c) $1 - (1 - 0.05)^3$ is the α per-family.

138. (d) since there are 5 means, there will be $(5 \times 4)/2 = 10$ comparisons. Thus adjusted p value will be $.006 \times 10 = .06$ which is greater than 0.05.

139. (a) Since there are 28 comparisons and we want 1% family-wise error, therefore corrected α should be (0.01)/28.

140. (b) As there are six comparisons and

$$\text{p(Bonferroni)} = 6 \times \text{p(LSD)}$$
$$\text{So p(LSD)} = .72/6 = 0.12$$

141. (c) As $Z > 1.65$ or $-Z < 1.65$ represents one tailed probability $p < .05$.

142. (a) Type I error is Rejecting a Null Hypothesis when it is in fact True. Similarly, Type II error is error in not rejecting a hypothesis when it should have been rejected. So both statements are false.

143. (c) The two tailed probability = 2(.09) = 0.18. Hence null hypothesis should not be rejected at 0 .05 level of significance.

144. (d) As Z = 2.38 > 1.96.

145. (d) As (a) is not proper, lower level is not mentioned once higher level has been mentioned. Options (b) and (c) are false.

146. (d) It is standardised Residual i.e (fo-fe)/$\sqrt{fe}$, adjusted for marginal sums, hence Chi Square is the answer.

147. (b) Wilcoxon Test requires data on a scale higher than Ordinal scale.

148. (a) Residual analysis is related to Chi-Square test.

149. (c) Mann Whitney test is used oncc k-sample test i.e Kruskal-Wallis Test gives significant results.

150. (d) None is different from other as each pair consists of a parametric test alongwith its non parametric counterpart.

151. (c) All others are about related samples.

152. (d) As the rest are test of closeness of an observed distribution to some theoretical distribution.

153. (b) It predicts direction. One cannot say that a directional hypothesis is positive.

154. (c) Although the hypothesis contains the word 'not', yet it is not a null hypothesis, since it essentially means that rural students are less anxious than urban students, the answer is (c).

155. (a) Since samples are related and more than two, it is Repeated Measure ANOVA. Trend Analysis is ruled out as within group effects are not intended.

156. (c) For, now the within group effects are required.

157. (c) Let us examine each statement: (a) is false as there can be a non-directional alternative hypothesis. (b) is ruled out as a null hypothesis need not be statistical. Since a statistical hypothesis has to be declarative, the answer is (c).

158. (a) It refers to an explanatory text.

159. (d) Obviously, I is wrong. II also, is false as it does not mention a statistic which is to be compared.

160. (d) Since covariate is statistically controlled variable in an experiment.

161. (c) As it states, in essence, that achievement with or without Reinforcement is not different.

162. (a) No difference between two groups (on same criterion variable).

163. (a) Obviously, all others are meaningless.

164. (b) Covariate affects dependent variable and confounds the effect of independent variables.

165. (a) It is an example of Casual-Comparative research.

166. (b) As duration of exam is independent variable manipulated by the experimenter.

167. (a) Casual-Comparative Research

168. (b) Clearly, it is experimental

169. (d) Note that in a parallel group design the second group is not given treatment, so answer is not (c). There is single group, some of the subjects have Central Vision Loss, others have Peripheral Vision Loss. Hence answer is (d).

170. (c) McNemar's Test is used in situation having replicated measures from a single group when data is on nominal scale having just two categories.

171. (c) As two tailed rejection area will be double of either tail area and will be situated either in the left or the right tail. These conditions are satisfied by (c) only.

172. (a) Not only F but t-test also utilises error variance in its formula.

173. (c) It states no difference between two variables, which is meaningless.

174. (d) It depends on the objective. One variable which is an independent variable in one objective may not be so in other objective. It may be dependent variable or even covariate.

175. (c) It affects dependent variable and that is why is controlled.

176. (a) Dependent variable is also termed as criterion variable.

177. (d) None of the statement is true.

178. (d) Not a null hypothesis. Also, both variables are correlates.

179. (d) As it is an alternative hypothesis and also no direction is predicted.

180. (a) Obviously enough.

181. (b) A Covariate i.e. concomitant variable is statistically controlled.

182. (d) No cause-effect relationship exists. So none is independent/dependent variable.

183. (c) As it is a grouping variable.

184. (b) As it is related to the generalizability of findings which may be jeopardised in view of excessive controls.

185. (c) Since b′ = r^2, it cannot happen that b and b′ have opposite signs (as r^2 is positive)

186. (d) Kindly see the above.

187. (d) since regression coefficient, of Y on X, $b = r\frac{\sigma y}{\sigma x}$

b can be zero, if r=0. Also, it can be negative if r is negative. It can also be greater than 1. So (d) is the answer.

188. (b) Residual SS indicates error in prediction, Thus Residual SS = $\Sigma(\tilde{Y} - Y)^2$.

189. (c) In case of no relationship between Y and X, the best prediction is $\bar{Y}$ i.e. $\tilde{Y} = \bar{Y}$. The quantity $\Sigma(\tilde{Y} - \bar{Y})^2$ shows how significant a regression is.

190. (b) As the two regression equations are identical only in case of perfect correlation between the two variables X and Y. So, statement II is correct in such eventuality. Statement I is false as both equations represent the same line.

$$Y = -1.5 + 0.5X \text{ and}$$
$$2Y = -3 + X \text{ or } 2Y + 3 = X \text{ are identical.}$$

191. (b) As actual values of Y are shown by points marked (x) and predicted values lie on the Regression line.

192. (c) As I does not lie on regression line.

193. (a) HL represents ($\bar{Y}$ – Y), it is not relevant to Residual SS.

194. (c) DE is the answer as D represents the actual value, whereas E is the predicted value.

195. (d) As Constant term is intercept of regression line on Y axis i.e. OA. Alternatively, Regression of Y on X is given by :

$$\tilde{Y} = a + bX$$

put $X = 0,$

$$\tilde{Y} = a,$$

so, it is the part of Y axis intercepted by the regression line.

196. (a) Since a = OA which is negative, Also, the slope of Regression line is positive, so b is positive. Hence answer is (a).

197. (c) $a = \tilde{Y} - bX$, so it depends on b.

198. (a) $SS_{Total} = SS_{Residual} + SS_{Regression}$

since $SS_{Regression} = 0$, $SS_{Total} = SS_{Residual}$

Hence, $SS_{Residual}$ cannot be zero.

199. (d) Let us take statement I first;

$t_{calculated} < t_{tabulated}$ (One tailed) , So H_0 cannot be rejected in favour of the directional hypothesis.

Now statement II is also false as predicted value of Y need not be zero in case a is zero.

200. Adjusted $\overline{Y} = \overline{Y} - b(\overline{X} - \overline{X}_{total})$

Adjusted $\overline{Y}$ will be adjusted upward when The quantity, $b(\overline{X} - \overline{X}_{total})$ is negative, i.e. when b is positive and $\overline{X} < \overline{X}_{total}$. Hence answer is (b).

The AUTHORS

Dr. S.K. Tyagi, a senior Professor of Education in School of Education, Devi Ahilya Vishwavidyalaya, Indore, has been teaching research and statistics to post graduate classes for the last more than twenty-five years. He has been a resource person in many workshops and refresher courses conducted on Research Methodology, Statistics and Use of SPSS, besides organising such workshops himself.
Prof. Tyagi has co-authored a book titled 'Test Your Understanding of Research and Statistics in Social Science' co-authored with Prof. D.N. Sansanwal. He has published more than thirty research papers in National and International journals of repute and has guided several Ph.D. students.

Dr. Shanti Tejwani obtained her Ph.D. in Education from School of Education, Devi Ahilya University, Indore on 'Comparison of Different Formats of Multiple Discriminant Items with Multiple choice Test Items'. She is currently Assistant Professor of Education in M.B. Khalsa Institute of Education, Indore. She has teaching experience of more than a decade to her credit. She has published many research papers in peer reviewed national journals and has attended a number of national conferences and workshops all over the country.

Ms. Kaushalya Khatri, a UGC, Junior Research Fellow in Education worked for her Ph.D. in Educational Evaluation from Devi Ahilya University, Indore. She has a keen interest in Measurement and Evaluation and Use of SPSS in research.